FORGIVE AND BE SET FREE

BY
APOSTLE LUDLOW HAYNES

FORGIVE AND BE SET FREE
Copyright © 2017 by **Apostle Ludlow Haynes**

ISBN: 978-1-957809-67-0

Printed in the United States of America. All rights reserved solely by the publisher. This book or parts thereof may not be reproduced in any form, stored in a retrieval system, or transmitted in any form by any means - electronic, mechanical, photocopy. Unless otherwise noted, Bible quotations are taken from the Holy Bible, New King James Version. Copyright 1982 by Thomas Nelson, Inc., publishers. Used by permission.

Published By:
Cornerstone Publishing, USA
A division of Cornerstone Creativity Group LLC
Info@thecornerstonepublishers.com
www.thecornerstonepublishers.com

Author's Information
Apostle Ludlow Haynes
Phone: 516:849-9625.
Email: Apostlehaynes50@gmail.com

Table of Contents

Chapter 1 5
    Forgiveness 5

Chapter 2 17
    Unforgiveness In Your Home 17

Chapter 3 31
    We Do Not Have To Live With Unforgiveness 31

Chapter 4 35
    Holding on to Unforgiveness 35

Chapter 5 43
    Renunciation of the Occult 43

Chapter 6 47
    Scriptures on Forgiveness 47

About the Author 55

CHAPTER 1
Forgiveness

What is Forgiveness? Forgiveness is the process of being pardoned. This simply means that you no longer have hurt, anger, pain, or disagreements with a person or an organization.

I have come to realize that a lot of relationships are broken because of unforgiveness in the heart, I also believe that the most dangerous disease a man could face is that of unforgiveness.

Let's take a look at how Jesus taught the disciples by saying the Lord's Prayer in Matthew: 6: 9-15 (NIV)

"This, then, is how you should pray: Our Father in heaven,
hallowed be your name,
your kingdom come,
your will be done,
on earth as it is in heaven.
Give us today our daily bread.
And forgive us our debts,
as we also have forgiven our debtors.
And lead us not into temptation,

but deliver us from the evil one.
For if you forgive other people when they sin against you, your heavenly Father will also forgive you.
But if you do not forgive others their sins, your Father will not forgive your sins."

Remember we were born in sin and shapened in iniquity, which means that we are in constant need of forgiveness from our fellow man and from God.

Sometimes we may wonder why is it that we struggle daily with our needs not being met, or why is it that we are suffering so much. Let us take a look at some of the issues that affect us;

1. Some of us have been hurt by someone we met for the very first time.
2. You may have been raped by a loved one or by a family member.
3. You probably were abused verbally or physically.
4. You may also suffer from rejection.

Let me tell you this, sometimes we do not have control over what is happening or what happened to us. Stop blaming yourself for all that happened or is happening to you. A path was made for us to escape unforgiveness and we need to take advantage of this.

Jesus has made a way for us to escape, He came and paid the price for our sins. He will take the place of all the hurts and pain that you are going through and gives you joy.

I know it is not easy for you to bear these sufferings when you have been raped and abused, it will take a toll on you emotionally, mentally and physically and will cause havoc on your health.

You must surrender these feelings to the Holy Spirit. If you do not, you will go around hurting people also, because "hurt people hurt people" and most times the cycle continues down to our children and others around us.

These feelings can make us oppressed, depressed and stressed to the point of wanting to commit suicide.

If we do not ask for forgiveness, how do we expect to be safe and secured from the harms of the enemy? If our hearts aren't pure, how can you lead others to Christ? How can God live in your heart if you are carrying around all these hurts, pains and rejections?

Psalm 66: 18 says

"If I had not confessed the sin in my heart, the Lord would not have listened." (NLT)

Our heavenly father would like to reason with us but how can He do that if we are so busy carrying around all the heavy burdens and baggage from our past?

Let's take a look at Isaiah 1: 19-20 NLT

"Come now, let's settle this,"
says the Lord.
"Though your sins are like scarlet,
I will make them as white as snow.
Though they are red like crimson,
I will make them as white as wool.
If you will only obey me,
you will have plenty to eat.
But if you turn away and refuse to listen,
you will be devoured by the sword of your enemies.
I, the Lord, have spoken!"

So, do you now understand why you still suffering, why your dreams and aspirations are failing?

You are going around complaining about how bad things are for you when God has given His instructions for you to follow and live a successful and bountiful life. For so many years you have been looking at the shooter and missing the Healer. Like the man at the pool of Bethsada, the angel of the Lord troubled the water, he couldn't get in because he was looking for someone to put him in the water, he missed the healer. The healer came along asking for his pain, the moment he gave up his pain he was made whole and receive his feet to walk.

It is time to get back your life, you have been living beneath standards, nothing is working in your favor! You can't keep a relationship because you are seeing through the eyes of rape, rejection, abuse and unforgiveness. You are blaming others, why not take the beam out of your eyes so you can see clearly that the problem is not your partner/family member or children, but it is in fact you, the problem is you.

Matthew 7: 4 NLT says " How can you think of saying to your friend, 'Let me help you get rid of that speck in your eye,' when you can't see past the log in your own eye?" Isn't this hypocritical?

Firstly, remove the speck (hurt, anger, pain, rejection, unforgiveness) from your eyes then you can help your brother to do the same.

Let's look at the lives of many people who are victims of rape and abuse, many of them change the natural use of the being attracted to the opposite sex to being attracted to the same sex. Like the women who changed the natural use of a man and turn to women which is unnatural. One of the reasons is because many were raped, so the devil used this situation to spread lesbianism and homosexual lifestyle in the world, but God's children are crying out for help! But where is the voice of the church?

God understands your struggles, so get up and fight the good fight of faith for your victory. Do not allow the Lord to be grieved with you because he extended his mercy towards you. Make use of the mercy.

He said in Romans 1:26-31

"For this reason God gave them up to vile passions.

For even their women exchanged the natural use for what is against nature. Likewise also the men, leaving the natural use of the woman, burned in their lust for one another, men with men committing what is shameful and receiving in themselves the penalty of their error which was due.

And even as they did not like to retain God in their knowledge, God gave them over to a debased mind, to do those things which are not fitting: being filled with all unrighteousness; full of envy, murder, strife, deceit, evil-mindedness; they are whisperers, backbiters, haters of God, violent, proud boasters, inventors of evil things, disobedient to parents, undiscerning, untrustworthy, unloving, unforgiving, unmerciful."

These are all spirits that operate in the lives of those that are victims of rape and abuse. The answer to your pain is Jesus! Receive him as your Lord and Savior.

2 Corinthians 5:17 said

"Therefore, if anyone is in Christ, he is a new creation; old things have passed away; behold, all things have become new."

My brother and sister obey the voice of God which is the word of God, be healed from your pain! You shall suffer no more! John 15:3:

" You are already clean because of the word which I have spoken to you,"

Don't be stubborn or stiff neck, it is no need for you to suffer like that because you refuse to obey God's word. Do you rather to die with your pain, shame and disobedience. The Lord said if you take heed to His word He will cleanse you of your shame. Psalm 119:9 " How can a young man cleanse his ways? By taking heed according to your word, now seek the Lord with your whole heart and do not wander from his commandment, the Lord will then keep you from death and destruction, you shall live again.

Many times in my walk of life, I have met various types of people like prostitute, alcoholic and mentally ill. I take the time out to speak and listen to them. I learnt to look beyond their faults and see their needs. "How can I help this person from taking their life or the life of another?" I then realized I am dealing with a big problem. It is a very sensitive situation. Sometimes the person carry themselves very shabby as if they gave up on themselves, this is a sign of low self esteem. They have gotten so low that they are ashamed of themselves and ashamed of what people think of and about them. They are trying to be accepted until they find themselves in the hands of another abuser. Why? Because spirit attracts spirit of its kind.

I also realized that there is a great need for deliverance because some people are so withdrawn from their partners and family members. No one understands what is going on and no one is trying to find out the reasons for withdrawal. At this crucial moment, they need someone to minister grace, that will help them in time of need. Remember they don't trust anyone at this moment and they do not want their secrets exposed because it seems very disgraceful, and that's the plan of the enemy to let you feel so guilty so that you will hold on to your past and be sick, angry, bitter, very unforgiving and can't prosper in life. Everything you start in life it will fail. This is because God said in Proverbs 28: 13 – 14

"He who covers his sins will not prosper, but whoever confesses and forsakes them will have mercy. Happy is the man who is always reverent, but he who hardens his heart will fall into calamity."

The Lord wants you to be happy because unhappiness is not only affecting you but also your children and other people that you involve in your pain, you cover yourself because of shame. You then expose someone else for destruction, you always paint a picture to your children as if someone else is the problem when you are the unhappy, hurt and resentful one. But because the children are so young and their minds are so frail, you do everything for them to get them believing in you, not knowing you are destroying them and sowing a legacy of evil and unforgiveness for them to carry on to the next generation.

Now, the love and respect is gone out of the family and your house, your children will become hateful of either mother and /or father. Both partners are not seeing eye to eye because one thinks the other person "needs my body" so it becomes a problem in the relationship. One is withholding from the other person because of money, sex, communication. Children lose respect for one of the parents. If God is fully accepted by both parents/partners as God, then He will hold everything together, and if the two are walking together and can't agree, it is now an open door for the devil's destruction. Who is to be blamed? The person who is holding the grudge in their hearts? You cannot have a successful relationship or home life if you are living a lie and rejecting the truth. Lie meaning that you are working with the devil because he is the father of lies and the truth is not in him.

Mothers and fathers, let us not produce any thieves, murderer and liars. We can produce holy children, but we must be holy as Christ is Holy. Come on... let us get it together- you know the tree by its fruit. A bad tree cannot bear good fruit, neither a good tree bear a bad fruit, so if you are the tree of life, how can you then produce fruit of hate, anger, malice, bitterness, unforgiveness and revenge, these fruits are not from the tree of life, but from the tree of death and that's the devil. The tree of life bear fruits like Love, Peace, Longsuffering, Joy and Togetherness. This type of tree produces good children and a good home, good attitude and good behavior. Don't let unforgiveness destroy your home right before your eyes! You can do something about it before it destroys your household. God will hold you responsible for destroying these little children's mind because they are wondering why their mothers or fathers have no peace among themselves. Parents always yelling and the house isn't burning down. What seems to be the problem? Someone heart is sick and they are taking it out on somebody and the children get caught in the middle, as a matter of fact, the children are isolating themselves because they don't understand what is going on and have to please the abuser because they are now scared. They are tired of hearing the shouting of anger and bitterness, so they try to please the abuser while suffering in their minds. Can't you see the damage you are doing to yourselves, husbands, wives and children? This must stop! Let us put the devil out of business in Jesus name!

I see people that are so abused by their past abusers, until they can't get over the pain and suffering. They become so depressed until they end up on depression medication. They act as if everything is ok with them until that demon reminds them of their past. They start having nightmares, withdrawal, yelling for no reason, continuous stress, lack of intimacy for your partner, isolating oneself for lack of communication, constant fear of being alone, sometimes or most of the times the abused becomes the abuser and your partner doesn't understand what is really going on because there is no communication to relate to your partner what is really going on in your life and how both of you can come together and deal with the matter. You rather allow the problem to stay and grow until it produces a break up in marriage or relationship and when this happens, the abuser always throw the blame on someone else. It is never their fault, it is always the fault of someone else. When are you going to take responsibility for your own actions? Are you going to kill your husband/wife, children or friends? Get your act together and allow Jesus in your life. Give him your hurts and pains by faith and He will heal you. Tell yourself you will not remain the victim of your past. You will not remain angry or bitter, you will not remain with guilt and shame. I now say to you that Jesus will cover your reproach with His blood, He will wash away your pain, shame, guilt, anger, unforgiveness and revenge. You don't have to hurt the person, forgive and be free.

Chapter 2
Unforgiveness In Your Home

Parents, if you see your children acting strange toward another child or they stop speaking as they used to, you should call them together, speak with them in love and confess our faults together and allow them to respond to you. If you know of a situation between siblings you should call them together and rectify the matter before you give an occasion to the devil to destroy the family. Can you imagine when King David heard that his daughter Tamar was raped by her own brother Amnom, he stepped in and called a meeting with them to restore them with the spirit of love and forgiveness.

Parents and children! Do not let the enemy enter your minds and homes to destroy what you worked so hard for. Some of you think that some sin is greater than some, but I just want to let you know that sin is sin – non greater, non less. So, when you hold the person's sins in your heart and keep putting it in their face, you are simply giving power to the devil. Just remember this, All have sinned and come short of the glory of God that my friend includes you and I. Maybe your daughter or son was raped, don't be like David and hold it against the perpetrator, forgive them, it happened out of ignorance. Remember what our Lord Jesus the Christ went through? The beatings, the torturing and the crucifixion and all He said at the end was " Father forgive them for they know not what they have done."

A lot of times in the homes when couples argue, they have little to no open communication, no relationship, no fellowship with each other. Something went wrong and they refuse to speak about it, instead, they sit on it and give the devil a foothold or a place to enter their lives and homes, Ephesians 4: 27. Why would you allow the devil to win your homes and relationships over? When Jesus already said to give him the battle and you will win the war! For this battle is not yours, it is the Lord's, so instead of hating your partner for the wrong they have done, why not love them so that you can fulfill the law of God, remember the Lord said in Romans 12:19: Leave vengeance to the Lord and He will repay. Do not take matters on your hands, you will have to pay for it on judgment day. As Proverbs 3:5 says you shouldn't lean on your own understanding, but in all thy ways acknowledge Him and He shall direct your path. All I'm saying to you is this, wait on the Lord, things might not happen quick enough for you, but remember that God is an on time God. He will use your pain to heal you so that you have a mighty testimony and experiences all over the world. Things may not look so great anymore, you thought you lost the love of your life, you thought you can never love again, but I am here to tell you that you can because you have God on the inside and God is love. When you love, you show that you are a child of God.

Forgiveness seems to be a hard subject for many people, but for God, it is the easiest thing to do. If we realize the damage it does to our health, wealth, relationships with our family members and friends we would forgive easily. Let me let you in on a little secret; this unforgiveness spirit knows how to cover up itself and expose others. This spirit plans to kill, destroy and steal the very joy of God out of one's life. This spirit is like a python that takes hold of his prey and squeeze the very life out of you, this spirit doesn't want to see you prosper. It doesn't like to see you get praise or recognition. This spirit is cunning and doesn't show itself in public because it doesn't want to be exposed to the light. It cries out in the night for its prey, it keeps company with other evil people who influence them to do wrong to their partners. Unforgiveness can disguise itself in any person or the best in people, however, the only way for you to find out is if you get close to them and start a conversation, then you will realize that they have a problem with their partners. Someone needs to reach out and help them because they do not think that they need help or they do not see that they are leading down to a path of destruction. This they can't see because the devil has blinded their eyes and minds and they can't see the danger they are doing to their families and themselves. If you are reading this book and it identifies with what you are going through, I implore that you get it right now before it is too late. Seek help from a counselor or a spiritual advisor before it costs you your home, family or life. Get rid of that spirit, surrender it to Jesus. Recognize what is going on in your life, it's not anybody trying to get you, it's the spirit of your past that you are holding on to. Let it go before it kills you mentally, emotionally, financially and spiritually. Let it go! This spirit doesn't like you and it is not of God, it is of the devil. God wants the best for you, so work with God in obedience and God will work with you.

Have you realized that you are crying too much and nothing is happening for you. This is because you are living in the darkness of your shame. It needs to be exposed and come to light, as long as you stay in the dark you are dwelling with demons, they will work on you until you hate yourself and even commit suicide. But it doesn't have to get that far for you to walk in the light. Which is Jesus, He is the light of the world.

2 Corinthians 5:17

"If any man be in Christ he is a new creature, old things are past away, and behold all things are new."

Remember Jesus came so that you may have life and life more abundantly, so choose life and live! Don't let the devil rob you of your birthright and your inheritance of the kingdom of God. He wants to mess with your mind and make you helpless. He wants you to know that you can't be successful in whatever you put your mind to. He is the father of Lies, don't you dare listen to him! Listen to Jesus, who is your true father. He said. "my sheep hear my voice and come and follow me, a stranger's voice they will not hear." Please don't allow the devil to speak in your ears, it is not good for you, it's only making you bitter, angry, resentful, having withdrawals, are unforgiving and revengeful. You just find yourself wanting to hurt the person that hurt you. That, my friend is not the plan that God has for you, you may believe in the popular saying " an eye for an eye and a tooth for a tooth" but that's not under God's law, you are now under God's grace which is a better covenant, just remember what He said in Romans 12:19; He will repay all those who hurt and abused you, all you have to do is turn it over to the Lord and he will fix it for you. Study the word of God and it will ease your pains also,

Ephesians 4:31

"And put away from you all bitterness, wrath, anger, loud shouting, evil speaking, with all malice."

God is saying that these are not good for you and your family. Do you ever wonder why you have no love for your mate, this is because you allow these demons to manifest and steal the joy that the Lord has given you or the rights you have in God. You are living more in your past than that of your future. It is time to put on love.

Ephesians 4:32

"And be ye kind one to another tenderhearted, forgiving one another, even as God for Christ's sake hath forgiven you."

My dear friend, it is up to you if you want to live for God or for the devil. Remember the devil represents death and Jesus represents life, so the choice is yours. Poor choice gets you poor results, whilst a right choice guarantees you healthy results. My friend I am asking you to take heed, Jesus wants what's best for you and so do I. In Deuteronomy 30:19 – I call heaven and earth as witnesses today against you, that I have set before you life and death, blessing and cursing; therefore choose Life, that both you and your descendants may live. With that being said you now know that your action of life can make or break you and your family. So it's up to you to change, God wants you to change but you have to forgive yourself. How can this be attainable you ask? In Psalm 199:9 it says " How can a man cleanse his way? By taking heed according to the word of God."

I was a messed up man on the inside and sin became my worst disease, it was slowly destroying me and I didn't know what to do or where to turn or even who to turn to. I was a destruction to myself and others. Persons tried showing me love, but I couldn't receive it. There are some of you right now who are reading this, you are so hurt in your home by family members, you have not felt love or have been loved by your parents, so now you put up a wall between your partner. You are fearful and you can't trust, so it's best you stay hurting and blaming others instead of working on your change. I know it's hard for us man to do it but with God all things are possible if you believe. Stop blaming yourself for what already happened. You have no control over that, you didn't ask for it but hey, things happen to the best of us. You can read the Bible and see of others who have been hurt, you will see how they overcame. They learnt how to seek the Lord with their whole hearts and there is where they found healing and deliverance and went on to live happily. This too can happen to you my friend, you are next in line for a miracle. Start reading the word of God for yourself. It is the best prescription and Jesus is the mighty physician. He prescribed John 15:3 for us, it says "You are already clean because of the word which I have spoken to you. Jesus said abide in me and I in you, if we do this it will be easy for him to take away our pain and hurt because we are drawing from a source that can never run dry. In him is the fruit of life.

The fruits of the spirit is Love, Joy, Peace, Longsuffering, Kindness, Goodness and Faithfulness, so now if you find yourself having difficulties in these, then it's not your partner, it is you. Come on my friend, take responsibility for your actions, break yourself away from the work of the flesh.

Galatians 5: 19 – 22

"Now the works of the flesh are evident, which are adultery, fornication, uncleanness, lewdness, idolatry, sorcery, hatred, contentions, jealousies, outbursts of wrath, selfish ambitions, dissensions, heresies, envy, murders, drunkenness, revelries, and the lake of which I tell you beforehand. Just as I also told you in time past, that those who practice such things will not inherit the kingdom of God. So if the kingdom is not meat and drink, but righteousness, peace and joy."

You see the reason why you don't have peace, love and joy is because you are living in the flesh. You cannot please God for they that are of the flesh can't please God and neither can he inherit from the kingdom of God. The kingdom is God, and everything that God is, man is entitled to because it is in him.

Get up out your slumber and sleep, your poverty and sickness and live in the spirit. If you live in the spirit, you will have life and peace.

Now this the word of the Lord, whose report will you believe? If God be God? Serve Him! You can't lose with Him, in Him is life and the life is the light of men.

John 1:14

"So let your light so shine before men that they may see your good works and glorify our father which is in Heaven."

You have work to do my friend. Stop glorifying the devil and start glorifying God! Stop giving power to the devil. Power belongs to God.

Matthew 28:18

"Jesus said to them, all authority and power has been given to me in heaven and earth."

God has made complete provision for your healing. Putting God's word to work I saw Him confirming that His word can produce healings and miracles. During my mission in the gospel, I heard of a woman who had a threatening lung condition. Her lungs were like leather and it was difficult for her to breathe. Someone shared with her and her husband what the word of God says about healing. They prayed in faith for her expecting to see the power of God and it began to make her whole. There was a strong presence of God as they were with her, yet she did not receive. It was as if she repelled God's healing instead of receiving it. They prayed several times, yet the results were the same. So they returned home asking God why she would not receive her healing. Then this scripture came to mind

Proverbs 18:14

"The spirit of a man will sustain his infirmity; but a wounded spirit who can bear?"

As I think on this verse, I believe that the Holy Spirit caused me to understand what this lady's problem was. Her spirit was deeply wounded. They went back to visit the lady and told her that God gave them a scripture for her, the same scripture, Proverbs 18:4. They went on explaining to her that one of the things that can wound our spirit is unforgiveness and that this unforgiveness could prevent her from receiving her healing. They asked her if she had unforgiveness towards someone. Her response was more than what they expected. She told them that when she was young, a well respected man in her community had physically taken advantage of her wheelchair bound grandmother. She swore as a child that she'd never forgive him and she still had hatred in her heart towards him. They asked her to forgive him but she said she couldn't do such a thing, she had tried before but she just couldn't. They eventually quieted her down and prayed for and with her, commanding that the spirit of unforgiveness and hatred go from her in the name of Jesus. They then lead her in prayer where she asked God to forgive her and to help her forgive this man for what he has done to her grandmother. Shortly after she began to cry with relief as God was working in her heart, the Holy Spirit took over and the lady and her husband began confessing their sins for the next 30 minutes; forgiving one another and receiving forgiveness from each other and God.

It was an amazing sight! They then prayed for her healing and there was a noticeable difference as she received the healing power of God and her breathing ability started to improve. I don't know the medical explanations as to how forgiveness upsets the chemical balance on our bodies, however, I do know that unforgiveness will give place to sickness and diseases in our bodies. It can also prevent us from getting better. The word of God speaks to us about unforgiveness in Matthew 18: 34-35

"And his lord was wroth, and delivered him to the tormentors, till he should pay all that was due unto him. So likewise shall my heavenly Father do also unto you, if ye from your hearts forgive not everyone his brother their trespasses."

So if we do not forgive our brothers and sisters, neither will our heavenly father forgive us. The great news is that we do not have to live with unforgiveness. God sent his son Jesus to the earth to take our sins from us and to provide us with forgiveness (and so much more). Not just forgiveness in a spiritual or religious sense, but cleansing so complete that it has no more effect on us.

1 John 1: 19

"If we confess our sins, He is faithful and just to forgive us and to cleanse us from all unrighteousness."

You may need to break free from unforgiveness and the entanglement of sin. If so, find someone who knows Jesus, who understands the word of God and the power He has given us in His name, they will be glad to get you free.

1 John 1: 7

"But if we walk in the light, as he is in the light, we have fellowship one with another, and the blood of Jesus Christ his Son cleanseth us from all sin."

Proverbs 28:13

"He that covereth his sins shall not prosper: but whoso confesseth and forsaketh them shall have mercy."

Whenever you meet the requirement of the kingdom and obey God's word, your heart will be so joyful that you have to share your testimony of God's goodness towards you. Psalm 103: 1-5 " Bless the Lord, oh my soul, and all that is within me bless His holy name. Bless the Lord oh my soul and do not forget his benefits; who forgives all your iniquities; who heals all thy diseases. Who redeems your life from destruction; who crowns you with loving-kindness and tender mercies; who satisfies your mouth with good things: so that your youth is renewed like the eagle's. No one fully understands why is it that some people are healed and some aren't. Still, experience has taught us there are barriers to healing that can be removed if we are willing to deal with them.

Here are five steps that you can use to heal your household from unforgiveness:
1. The baptism of the Holy Spirit.
2. Seek revelation from God as what may be the barriers.
3. We must be honest with what God reveals to us.
4. We must then seek forgiveness from God and
5. Then we seek forgiveness from man.

When we seek forgiveness from everyone including ourselves we will also gain deliverance from the influence of evil spirits.

Here is a declaration I would like us to say out loud and believe with our whole hearts.

Declaration to Satan by Derek Prince based on Psalm 118:17

"I shall not die but live and declare the works of the Lord.

My body is the temple of the Holy Spirit, Redeemed, Cleanse and Sanctified by the Blood of Jesus.

My members and the parts of body are instruments of righteousness for His service And for His Glory.

The devil has no place in me, it has been settled by the Blood of Jesus.

I overcome Satan by the Blood of Jesus and by the word of my testimony and I love Not my life unto the death Amen!

Chapter 3
We Do Not Have To Live With Unforgiveness

Jesus came to earth to take our sins for us and to provide forgiveness. Not just forgiveness in a spiritual or religious sense, but cleansing so complete that it has no more effects on us.

You may need to break free from unforgiveness and the entanglement of sin. If so, find someone who knows Jesus. Someone who understands the Word of God and the power He has given us in His Name. They will be more than happy to help you get the freedom you deserve.

Here are some scriptures to direct us into forgiveness;

1 John 1:9

"If we confess our sins, He is faithful and just to forgive our sins, and to cleanse from all unrighteousness."

1 John 1: 7

"But if we walk in the Light, as He is in the light, we have fellowship one with another, and the blood of Jesus Christ His son cleanses us from all sins."

Proverbs 28:13

"He that covers his sin shall not prosper; but whoever confesses and forsakes them shall have mercy."

Psalm 103:1-5

Bless the Lord, O my soul: and all that is within me, bless his holy name. Bless the Lord, O my soul, and forget not all his benefits: Who forgiveth all thine iniquities; who healeth all thy diseases; Who redeemeth thy life from destruction; who crowneth thee with lovingkindness and tender mercies; Who satisfieth thy mouth with good things; so that thy youth is renewed like the eagle's.

Not only are we holding back ourselves, but we are also withholding our blessings that were promised to us from generations before and new promises that God said he will deliver unto us.

Can a Christian have a Demon?

Before we get into this, let us make another declaration over our lives. This declaration is a way to expel evil spirits.

Satan: I testify to you personally what the Word says the shed blood does for me in Revelation 12:11.
I (insert name) have been redeemed through the blood of Jesus and my sins are forgiven according to the richness of His Grace which is found in Ephesians 1: 7.
Through the blood of Jesus, all my sins are forgiven!

Giving thanks to the father which has made us to be partakers of the
Inheritance of the saints in Light: who has delivered us from the power of darkness, and has
Translated us into the kingdom of his dear Son, in who we have
Redemption through his blood, even the forgiveness of sins.
The shed Blood of Jesus is cleansing me now from all sins!
I am justified, made righteous, just as if I'd never sinned through the blood of Jesus.
And now I will be saved from wrath through Jesus the Christ, Amen!

Since physical affliction can be caused by an evil spirit, whether we are aware of any presence or not, this possibility should not be overlooked. If deliverance- the expelling of demons is needed, nothing else will suffice.

If this is not the case, there are no adverse consequences from acting on the possibility anyway. Jesus was appointed by God himself to go throughout the earth ministering and healing those who were oppressed by the devil. I am not saying that we should go out and look for demons to expel. But we should be aware of our surroundings and know how to sensitize and approach them.

CHAPTER 4
Holding on to Unforgiveness

Not forgiving is possibly the greatest barrier to healing, because the next barrier cannot be removed until this unforgiveness is removed.

Jesus said "If ye forgive men their trespasses, your heavenly father will also forgive you; but if ye do not forgive men their trespasses, neither will your father forgive your trespasses" Matt. 6: 14-15. This is a solemn warning that is commonly overlooked, even by zealous christians. The real problem with the sin of unforgiveness is that it is an ongoing condition of a person's heart.

Let's look at some of the reasons for a person having an unforgiving spirit.

SELF LOVE

Unforgiveness can result from self love. When we love ourselves more than others including our enemies, and when someone else sins against us, this in essence is self love. Self Love says "how dare you sin against me?"

God commands us to love our neighbors and even our enemies. Love is greater than faith. Love is greater than hope and even if you have the gift of prophecy; one of the greatest spiritual gifts and do not have love, you are nothing. -1st Corinthians 13: 2

1 Corinthians 13: 7

"Love beareth all things, believeth all things, hopeth all things, endureth all things."

Unforgiveness is proof of a lack of genuine love in your heart. One sad thing about harboring the sin of unforgiveness in your heart is **YOU ARE THE LOSER,** now and for eternity.

We have the power to be victorious beyond our imagination because the plans of the enemy is mostly repetitive.

2 Corinthians 2: 11

"So that Satan will not outsmart us. For we are familiar with his evil schemes."

Matthew 18: 21-23

Then Peter came to him and asked, "Lord, how often should I forgive someone who sins against me? Seven times?"
"No, not seven times," Jesus replied, "but seventy times seven!
"Therefore, the Kingdom of Heaven can be compared to a king who decided to bring his accounts up to date with servants who had borrowed money from him."

The reason Jesus commanded us to ask for forgiveness so many times is because it will no longer be a problem or an issue to us. We will no longer have hatred or hurt in our hearts if we forgive an act or hurt 490 times.

We should do this just as the Word of God says, seeing that we are to be seen as Christ is seen, we can see this in Ephesians 4: 32

"Instead, be kind to each other, tenderhearted, forgiving one another, just as God through Christ has forgiven you."

Colossians 3: 13

"Make allowance for each other's faults, and forgive anyone who offends you. Remember, the Lord forgave you, so you must forgive others."

We should ponder on these scriptures daily and hide them in our hearts as God instructs us to do. But, the decision is ours, it's an act of our will in obedience to Christ.

Here is a simple prayer you can say when you are ready to forgive:

Lord, I have a confession to make; there are certain people I have resented and I call upon you now to help me forgive them.
Lord Jesus, I do now, in obedience to your word and by an act of my will, forgive the following persons for anything they have ever done to hurt or disappoint me. (Now ask the Holy Spirit to bring to mind the names of every person living or dead that we need to forgive)

I also forgive myself Lord Jesus.
I thank you Lord Jesus!
I ask you to help me change any negative feelings I have had towards others and heal me of anything that has been a consequence of my disobedience to your Word by holding on to unforgiveness.

Another thing we can do is to be bold and apologize (to them) and ask for them to forgive us. Whether or not they forgive us or not, that is up to them. But we as christians should ask God to bless them every time we pray.

UNCONFESSED SINS

Any sin that has not been confessed, repented of, renounced or has been forgiven is a barrier to healing, this especially applies to healing of the mind, emotions and memories, since many physical healing will follow, scripture says that God will not listen to the prayer of those who continue to hold this iniquity in their hearts. Any disobedience to God or sin that is not dealt with in an open door for an evil spirit.

Psalm 66: 18

"If I had not confessed the sin in my heart, the Lord would not have listened."

The thing that got my attention was the subject matter: bitterness and unforgiveness. Really, I have managed to not allow these roots to develop in me. My family and friends had hurt me and I dealt with it by working extremely hard to forget it, on the principle that it does me no good to mull and remember them.

Remembrance of hurts for me is bad because it re awakens the old man (flesh). You see vengeance and anger were issues for me before I became a new creation in Christ Jesus. I worked extremely hard to have the new man nature of my spirit to be supreme of the yet unredeemed flesh that still houses my spirit and soul. The difficulty you and I have is forgetting, and in life there is something that triggers a memory, thus challenging us to forget. So, renew and transform your mind by reading and studying the Word of God. The Bible says "How can a man cleanse his ways, is by taking heed to the word of God. (Psalm 119:9).

The Bible also says in John 15: 3 "Now ye are clean through the word which I have spoken unto you."

Proverbs 28:13

"He that covereth his sins shall not prosper: but whoso confesseth and forsaketh them shall have mercy."

As the scripture outlines we need to put away pride and expose our sins so that we can serve God in spirit and in truth and live. I can assure you that you are not living the life that are supposed to be living right now because you are bitter, angry. I can also say that once persons speak objectively about an issue you think that they are speaking about you. You see, holding on to unforgiveness is like having a sore that is never treated, it gets worse and worse as the days goes by and guess what it also has an awful smell! This is exactly how unforgiveness is... the more we hold on to it the worse it gets. Speaking of sores; God is our doctor and we are refusing treatments, we cover up the sore and pretend that all is well. He is there offering us love and forgiveness but we cannot accept it because we have held steadfast to our unforgiveness, neither can we accept love from our fellow man. We are fearful of giving and accepting love also because we are afraid of being hurt.

Remember, not every person is the same, because you got hurt from someone doesn't mean that everybody else is still the same. Sometimes we pray for husbands or wives and God sends them along the way but we are so hurt and bitter that we push them away. We need to work on ourselves, we need to seek God our doctor who can cleanse our sores and dress them the proper way so that our happiness can come back, our health and wealth may come back and our full healing of mind, body and soul can be reactivated.

As christians we are supposed to be helping others, tell me how can you help someone while you are hurting. Can you give someone to drink from an empty, dirty cup? No you can't! You will even go as far as to find others who are hurting and group together because you want to dwell and roll in your unforgiveness. You don't want to be corrected. But let me tell you this, this is the plan of the enemy. This is the plan of the enemy to divide us so that he can conquer. You will also believe that your friends are better than you. These are the plans of the enemy, you don't need to compare yourself with others. Be yourself, be what God made you to be, be the best you in God and he will bless you with all spiritual and physical blessings.

All power belongs to God and He gives power to the church; which is you and I. Why then are you living in poverty, moving from shelter to shelter like a homeless person? Why can't you own a home? You see, unforgiveness can sometimes be the cause of these things.

Let me break this down for you... someone hurt or disappointed you; this is something that happened, this is something that is of the past. This is no more... it is behind you.

Why are you holding on to the past? Don't you see how you are hurting your children... filling them with pain and anguish. They can't live their own lives because they are too busy worrying and concerned about you. It also affects them as they grow older, this plays out in their personal relationships because you didn't show how to love in the home, you didn't teach them how to forgive, so their marriages end in divorce because of bitterness and unforgiveness. This my friend is what we call "repeating the curse." They blame everyone else for their failures and mistakes instead of taking responsibility for their actions and in turn abusing your partner. How long will you carry this secret with you? When will you let you partner in on what's happening to you? When will you turn it over to the Lord for him to deliver you? How much more of your joy are you going to let the devil steal from you? Don't you realize our, health and wealth is diminishing?

It's time for you to open up! It's time for to get help, time to speak to a professional who can help you to get over all this hurt and pain.

You have the power to do so, God gave you the power to trample all hurt, pain, shame and failure under your feet. You are above it! You are the head and not the tail! You can be in control!

Luke 10:19

"Behold, I give unto you power to tread on serpents and scorpions, and over all the power of the enemy: and nothing shall by any means hurt you."

This is a true statement. God has given us an escape, so we must and should use it at all times.

Chapter 5
Renunciation of the Occult

Any involvement in the occult is an abomination to God. Even a trivial interest in these areas can have severe and prolonged consequences. It is important to understand that we can renounce occult involvement for ourselves and from our ancestors who may have been in any of these practices. Sometimes we may find out that there are generational curses that have been passed down to us and we may begin to develop hatred and unforgiveness. We develop hatred and unforgiveness because things are not going well for us in our lives, everything seems to be going downhill.

But here is the good news about all of this;

Numbers 14: 18

"The Lord is slow to anger, abounding in love and forgiving sin and rebellion. Yet he does not leave the guilty unpunished; he punishes the children for the sin of the fathers to the third and fourth generation"

Deuteronomy 18:10-12

Let no one be found among you who sacrifices their son or daughter in the fire, who practices divination or sorcery, interprets omens, engages in witchcraft,
or casts spells, or who is a medium or spiritist or who consults the dead.
Anyone who does these things is detestable to the Lord; because of these same detestable practices the Lord your God will drive out those nations before you.

Dear Lord I have a confession to make, through ignorance, or willfulness I have sought supernatural experiences apart from you. I have disobeyed your word and I ask you to deliver me as I renounce all these things. Cleanse me in my mind body and soul I pray;

- I renounce for myself and my ancestors all contact with witchcraft, magic, ouija boards and other occult games.
- I renounce for me and my ancestors all kinds of fortune telling, palm reading, tea leaves reading, crystal balls, tarot card and other card laying.
- I renounce myself and ancestors all astrology, birth signs and horoscopes.
- I renounce myself and my ancestors the heresy of reincarnation and all healing groups involved in metaphysics and spiritualism.
- I renounce for myself and my ancestors all hypnosis under any excuse or authority.

- I renounce for myself and my ancestors, music that in any way is contrary to the word of God.
- I renounce for myself and my ancestors all transcendental meditation, and all other eastern cults and idol worship.
- I renounce for myself and my ancestors that all martial arts, including Judo, Kung Fu and Karate that in any way convey supernatural power that is not from God.
- I renounce for myself and my ancestors all water witching or dowsing, levitation, table tipping, psychometry (divination through objects).
- I renounce for myself and my ancestors all literature I have ever read and studied in any of these fields. I promise I will destroy all such materials in my possession.
- I renounce for myself and my ancestors astral projection and any other demonic skills.
- I renounce for myself and my ancestors in the Name of The Lord Jesus Christ all psychic power that I may have inherited and break any demonic hold or curse over my family line back to ten or more generations on both sides of my family.
- I renounce and forsake for myself and my ancestors every psychic and occult contact that I am unaware of, as well as those I may have forgotten.

- I renounce for myself and my ancestors every occult that denies atonement through the Blood of Jesus Christ and every philosophy that denies His deity.
- I promise to destroy any occult paraphernalia that I posses since they are an abomination.

Now satan! I cast down any strong holds that these activities may have established and close any door I may have opened to you through these contacts. I decree and declare that these cycles stop right now!

I declare that going forward there will be generational blessings!

I declare that my children and their children and their children's children will no longer have any ties to these as they have been renounced and will no longer be a part of our lives in Jesus name I pray, Amen!

As we have just renounced all these things; we now see how unforgiveness comes to play within each – from generation to generation. But no worries, you just put a stop to it.

Forgiveness has now gained clarity in your mind, body, soul and spirit.

CHAPTER 6
Scriptures on Forgiveness

Ephesians 4: 31- 32

"Let all bitterness and wrath and anger and clamor and slander be put away from you, along with all malice. Be kind to one another, tenderhearted, forgiving one another, as God in Christ forgave you."

Hebrews 12:14-15

"Strive for peace with everyone, and for the holiness without which no one will see the Lord. See to it that no one fails to obtain the grace of God; that no "root of bitterness" springs up and causes trouble, and by it many become defiled;"

Proverbs 20: 22

"Do not say, 'I will repay evil'; wait for the Lord, and he will deliver you."

Proverbs 10: 12

"Hatred stirs up strife, but love covers all offenses."

Luke 17: 3-4

"Pay attention to yourselves! If your brother sins, rebuke him, and if he repents, forgive him, and if he sins against

you seven times in the day, and turns to you seven times, saying, 'I repent,' you must forgive him."

I John 2: 9-11

"Whoever says he is in the light and hates his brother is still in darkness. Whoever loves his brother abides in the light, and in him there is no cause for stumbling. But whoever hates his brother is in the darkness and walks in the darkness, and does not know where he is going, because the darkness has blinded his eyes."

1 John 1: 9

"If we confess our sins, he is faithful and just to forgive us our sins and to cleanse us from all unrighteousness."

Ephesians 4: 32

"Be kind to one another, tenderhearted, forgiving one another, as God in Christ forgave you."

Mark 11: 25

"And whenever you stand praying, forgive, if you have anything against anyone, so that your Father also who is in heaven may forgive you your trespasses."

2 Corinthians 2" 10-11

"Anyone whom you forgive, I also forgive. Indeed, what I have forgiven, if I have forgiven anything, has been for your sake in the presence of Christ, so that we would not be outwitted by Satan; for we are not ignorant of his designs."

1 John 4: 20

"If we confess our sins, he is faithful and just to forgive us our sins and to cleanse us from all unrighteousness"

James 5: 16

"Therefore, confess your sins to one another and pray for one another, that you may be healed. The prayer of a righteous person has great power as it is working."

Matthew 18: 21-23

"Then Peter came up and said to him, 'Lord, how often will my brother sin against me, and I forgive him? As many as seven times?" Jesus said to him, "I do not say to you seven times, but seventy times seven. "Therefore the kingdom of heaven may be compared to a king who wished to settle accounts with his servants."

Encouragement to all my readers; you have to forgive right now before your heart becomes hard towards the individual who had hurt you. Do it quickly, it will eat away your health, your relationship with your family and also your coworkers. It will also make you angry and upset at everything, it will rob you of your joy in the Lord and your relationship with Him. you will lose all access to God's throne when you pray, the Lord will not listen to you because you regard iniquity in your heart.

Please remember that your heart is so vital to God that if it is not clean the Lord can't live there, so you have a job to do; guard your heart, for out of it flows the issue of Life. Matthew

15:19 states, that all your evil problems come from your heart, which is fornication, theft, adultery, murder, blasphemy, gossip, talebearing, hatred and malice. With a heart like this your prayer will not be answered because the Lord can't look at sin. Please follow the footsteps of David; he said unto God when he realized that his heart was his greatest problem, he cried "Lord, create in me a clean heart and renew a right spirit in me, take not thy Holy Spirit from me." This should be your cry, many people are crying about their problems, pains, past, the abuse of rape, the abandonment of husband or wife, the loss of a daughter, son, mother, father, grandmother or grandfather. it is time to let go of those things that you are crying about and move on with your life, cry unto the Lord like David, watch God turn your mourning into dancing, your sorrow into joy, your tears into laughter, your pain into healing, your mess into a message, your weakness into strength, your ashes into beauty, your downward into upward and your zero into hero. You need to see yourself as an overcomer, a victor, more than a conqueror in God. If any man be in Christ, he is a new creature, old things are passed away and behold all things are new, it is not enough just to change, a tadpole can change into a frog and a caterpillar can change into a butterfly, but God can make you into a new creation. Get out of your problems and get into Christ Jesus- your life.

Christ is the world answer for a new life, being outside of Christ is very dangerous for everyone because the devil is roaming the earth, by going up and down seeking whom he may devour. It is you and I, outside of Christ that are open to destruction. He comes to kill, steal and destroy. In Christ you are covered and protected, the devil can't find where you are. For the Bible said, "He that dwelleth in the secret place of the Most High shall abide under the shadow of the Almighty." You are now safe, no need to be afraid of the shadow by day nor the pestilence that lurk at noonday. God shall give angels charge to watch over you and your family because you made the best decision of your life; to escape from the devil and the world system and return to God. May I ask you a very serious and important question- What will it profit you to gain the whole world and lose your own soul. Is that what you want for your life? Jesus is calling you to a better place in Him, a place of peace, joy, happiness, success and prosperity.

When life dealt you a hard blow, try God a second time- I guarantee you will not regret it, it will be the best time of your life. You may ask; how am I so confident? This is because I have proven Him, and today I am what heaven intended for me to be. i'm a new creature, preaching the Gospel of the Kingdom with signs and wonders, following with lots of miracles, so examining yourself is very important, ensure your heart is clean and undefiled from any impurities of life. Remember Jesus is holy and so you and I have to be holy. Jesus said "Be ye Holy for I am Holy." He wants to live in His children, but we have some cleaning up to do before we welcome Him in. We have to make him comfortable so He can reign within and use us for His glory. He said "present your bodies as a living sacrifice; Holy and Acceptable unto me which is your reasonable service." Are you ready to give yourself up to God totally and completely? You will make the right choice, God is waiting with his arms wide open to supply every need in your life. Get ready for what He is about to do.

You would have to be blind, deaf and dumb to believe that you can live without God or His instructions. We have done so many wrong in our lives and are in need of God's forgiveness but the Lord can't meet our demands if we don't meet His requirement. Consider your ways, look into yourself and see if your life is going against what God stands for. If you are doing what He hates, He doesn't hate you He hates what you're doing and there are consequences for these actions; both on earth and in heaven. So now you are indebted and this debt you cannot pay. Jesus is ready to drop your charges by paying off your debt in full and redeem you of bondage and also give you liberty. Your job now is to stand fast in liberty where Christ has set you free and not to be entangled in the yolk of bondage. He said " If you forgive men their trespasses, your heavenly father will forgive you your trespasses.

What a day when the Lord frees us from our past and gives us a brand new future.

Forgiveness worked for me and it will definitely work for you. Oh happy day when Jesus fixed my life, He taught me how to watch and pray and live rejoicing every day, O Happy Day! I am Free!

About the Author

Ludlow Haynes was born 1964 in Manchester, Jamaica West Indies. He grew with his grandmother where it was a must to attend school and church.

At the age of 12, he migrated to Rae Town, Kingston 16, where he was exposed to gang violence and drugs and became a delinquent.

Ludlow then migrated to the U.S. at age 19 where he continued with the same delinquent lifestyle. He then got in deep trouble where he was faced with three guns to his head and saw his best friend dying in front of him. He got out of this dilemma because he had a praying mother and grandmother; whom God used to pray for him so that he would not die.

Down the road, Ludlow got stopped by police who then did some checks on him. He was going to be sentenced to 25 years in prison. His mother got the best lawyer and the sentence got reduced to six months and five years probation.

While imprisoned he had an encounter with the Lord. As soon he got released, he went to church with his mother. After serving for 10 years under that leadership, God called Ludlow to ministry in 2001.

Since then, Ludlow has been serving the Lord with great joy where he is the Pastor of Tabernacle of Victory in Franklin Square New York.

Ludlow is Married to the beautiful Cecile for 30 years where they 10 wonderful children and numerous grandchildren.

Made in the USA
Middletown, DE
08 August 2025